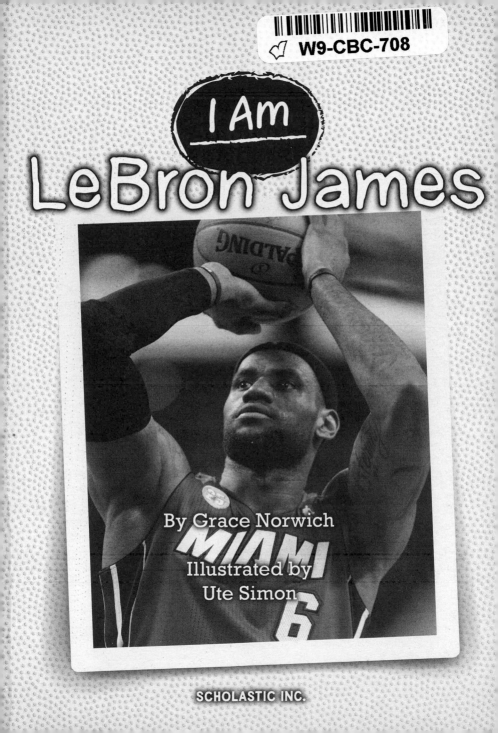

I Am
LeBron James

By Grace Norwich

Illustrated by
Ute Simon

SCHOLASTIC INC.

PHOTO CREDITS

Photographs © 2014: Akron Beacon Journal: 8 bottom left, 9 top, top right, 45 top right, bottom right, 46 (Robin Sallie); AP Images: 101 (Alex Menendez), 4, 8 bottom left, 44, 92 (Amy Sancetta), 50, 57 (Bruce Schwartzman), 83 (Charles Krupa), 107 (David Santiago), 117 (Eric Gay), 6 (Matt Slocum), 1 (Michael Dwyer), 110 (Mike Segar), 9 center (Paul Sancya), 52 (Paul Sancya), 8 top left (Phil Long), 17 (Phil Long); AP Images: 8 top (Tom DiPace), 9 bottom left, bottom, 95, 98, 114 (Tom DiPace), 102, 105 (Wilfredo Lee); Dreamstime: 54 (Agent87), 48 center right (Cugianza84), 70 (Nmarques74), 67 (Ratmandude), 11 (Spopho), 84 (Spopho), 69 (Zhuangmu); Getty Images: 118 (Al Bello), 9 center left, 87 (Alexander Tamargo), 113 (David Liam Kyle/NBAE), 96 (Gregory Shamus), 23 (J.D. Pooley), 42, 58 (Linda Spillers), 91 (Michael J. LeBrecht II/Sports Illustrated), 41 (Sergio Perez-IOPP Pool), 31, 49 (Stephen Dunn); iStock 48 (dell640), top right (Francesco Santalucia), 27 (Henryk Sadura), 61 (herreid), 24 (JaysonPhotography), 20 (Jitalia17), 32 (joebelanger),14 (JonGorr), 74 (littleny), 34 (lutherhill), 78 (Randall Esulto), 77 (sierrarat); LeBron James Foundation: 8 left center, 35, 38; Newscom: 62 (Phil Masturzo KRT); The Official White House Photo: 13 (Sonya N. Hebert).

UNAUTHORIZED: This book is not sponsored by or affiliated with LeBron James.

ISBN 978-0-545-79428-2

10 9 8 7 6 5 4 3 2 1   14 15 16 17 18 19/0

Printed in the U.S.A.   40
First printing, September 2014

Cover illustration by Mark Fredrickson
Interior illustrations by Ute Simon

CONTENTS

INTRODUCTION

I've been a pretty good basketball player ever since I was a teenager—well, maybe more than pretty good. My nickname, "King James," is used by my teammates, fans, and the media. But if you knew me before I was famous, that title might seem like a joke.

While I was growing up, my mom and I were so poor that we often found ourselves without a roof over our heads. We found shelter with friends and family in my hometown of Akron, Ohio. We slept on couches until it was time to move on. During this difficult time, my mom kept me on track. She isn't just the only parent I've ever had—she's also my best friend.

Long before I became one of the greatest basketball players, Kobe Bryant and Shaquille O'Neal were among the thousands of fans who showed up to watch me play power forward for my high-school team. I was just a shy kid with a special talent. Not even my mom, who believed in me from day one, could imagine the success that was waiting for me.

I didn't do it alone. I had the help of devoted coaches, who gave me a shot at greatness as well as a place to live when I really needed it. With *a lot* of hard work, I went from a gangly boy who liked to ride his bike alone around

the crumbling streets of Akron to a celebrated athlete on the cover of *Sports Illustrated* magazine.

The early lessons I learned about loyalty can be seen on the basketball court. I pass the ball as often as I shoot. My commitment to teamwork has helped me win championships as well as gold medals at the Olympics.

I may be basketball royalty, but I worked hard to earn my crown. I am LeBron James.

PEOPLE YOU WILL MEET

LEBRON JAMES
One of the best professional basketball players of all time. He overcame many obstacles to become a champion.

Gloria James: LeBron's mother, who lives in Ohio, was a single mom at a young age, and his biggest supporter.

Frankie Walker Sr.: A youth football coach who took in LeBron until he was ten and became an inspiring figure in LeBron's life.

Dru Joyce II: Coach of the Shooting Stars, who helped develop LeBron's on-court skills.

Dru Joyce III: LeBron's good friend and teammate on the Shooting Stars, known for his short height and shy demeanor.

Sian Cotton: LeBron's friend and teammate on the Shooting Stars, known for his practical jokes.

Willie McGee: LeBron's third friend and teammate on the Shooting Stars, known for his maturity and gifted ball handling.

Keith Dambrot: The head basketball coach at St. Vincent-St. Mary High School who helped LeBron learn discipline on and off the court.

Savannah Brinson: LeBron's high-school sweetheart, who became his wife when they married in 2013.

Chris Bosh: Power forward and center who currently plays with LeBron for the Miami Heat.

Dwyane Wade: Guard for the Miami Heat who—along with LeBron and Chris Bosh—is part of the group known as the "Big Three."

TIME LINE

- **December 30, 1984** – LeBron Raymone James is born to Gloria James in Akron, Ohio.

- **1994** – LeBron discovers organized team sports, playing Pee Wee football with the South Rangers and rec league basketball with the Summit Lake Hornets.

- **1996** – LeBron joins the Amateur Athletic Union, playing for the Shooting Stars. There he meets three players who become his lifelong friends.

- **1996–1999** – The Shooting Stars win an amazing six national championships.

September 1999 – Along with his three best friends from the Shooting Stars, LeBron begins attending St. Vincent-St. Mary High School, where he plays basketball *and* football.

1999-2003 – During his freshman, sophomore, and senior years, his high-school basketball team wins the state championships, and LeBron becomes a national star.

June 26, 2003 – The Cleveland Cavaliers select LeBron as the first pick in that year's NBA draft, held at Madison Square Garden in New York City.

- **2004** – LeBron is named NBA Rookie of the Year.

- **August 28, 2004** – LeBron plays on the U.S. Men's Olympic Basketball team in the Athens Olympic Games.

- **October 6, 2004** – LeBron James, Jr., is born to LeBron and his girlfriend, Savannah Brinson.

- **June 7–14, 2007** – The Cavaliers make it to the NBA Finals for the first time in the team's history.

- **June 14, 2007** – LeBron and Savannah's second son, Bryce Maximus, is born.

- **August 10–24, 2008** – LeBron and the U.S. Men's Olympic Basketball Team win gold at the Beijing Olympic Games.

- **July 8, 2010** – As a free agent, LeBron announces that he will sign with the Miami Heat, a decision that angers fans in his home state of Ohio.

- **June 21, 2012 –** The Miami Heat win the NBA championship and LeBron wins the Most Valuable Player (MVP) award.

- **August 12, 2012 –** LeBron and the U.S. Men's Olympic Basketball Team win gold at the London Olympic Games.

- **June 20, 2013 –** The Heat win the NBA championship and LeBron is MVP for a second time.

- **September 14, 2013 –** LeBron and Savannah get married in San Diego, California.

LeBron with Michelle Obama, Olympics 2012

Akron, Ohio

CHAPTER ONE

THE HOUSE ON HICKORY STREET

LeBron James and his mother, Gloria, have always been close. In fact, he likes to call her his best friend. Their connection began on the cold winter morning of December 30, 1984, when Gloria gave birth to LeBron in the working-class city of Akron, Ohio.

Life wasn't easy. Gloria was only sixteen years old when she had LeBron. LeBron's father was already gone when LeBron entered the world. As LeBron later put it, Gloria was

Gloria always took care of LeBron.

"my mother, my father, everything." At that time, their community was filled with crime, drugs, and **poverty**. Unemployment was high in Akron. "We had some tough times," the basketball star has

Gloria James

admitted, "but she was always there for me."

For the first few years of his life, LeBron and Gloria lived in a big house their family owned on Hickory Street. They lived with his grandmother, great-grandmother, and two uncles on a dirt road next to the railroad tracks. Grandmother Freda spent a lot of time taking care of little LeBron, but everyone helped, even his nine-year-old uncle, Curt. Although the James family didn't have much money, they showered LeBron with love, and he grew into a bouncy, athletic toddler.

A Life-Changing Christmas

In 1987, the year LeBron turned three, Christmas was marked by both joy and pain. Gloria and her boyfriend, Eddie Jackson, bought LeBron a child's basketball set. When Eddie and Gloria raised the level of the hoop as high as it would go, LeBron didn't shoot the ball into the basket like they thought he would. Instead, he took a running start, leapt up, and slam-dunked the ball. When Eddie saw this, he must have thought, *This toddler really has game*.

However, LeBron's world changed on the night of Christmas Eve. At three a.m., LeBron's beloved grandmother suffered a massive heart attack and passed away at their Hickory home.

Tough Times

Soon, the family really began to struggle. Gloria and her brothers tried to maintain the house on Hickory Street, but it was too old, too

LeBron showed an early talent for basketball.

An eviction notice
on a home

big, and too expensive. Even with food and
babysitting help from neighbors, Gloria and
her brothers couldn't afford to pay for the heat,

and the house started to fall apart. There was a hole right in the middle of the floor, which was getting bigger by the day. Eventually, the city **condemned** the house, and the James family had to move. With only a single suitcase and his favorite blue stuffed elephant, LeBron and his mom left the only home he had ever known.

THE CITY THAT RUBBER BUILT

Located approximately forty miles south of Cleveland, Akron, Ohio, was once known as the "rubber capital of the world" because big companies such as Goodyear and Firestone made millions of tires in the city's factories. By the time LeBron was born, most of those companies had moved their business elsewhere. When the tire industry of Akron moved its business overseas, thousands of manufacturing jobs were lost overnight. That negatively affected the entire city. Without jobs, people didn't have money to shop in stores or buy houses. Many people had to move away from Akron in search of work and those who stayed had little opportunity. The damaging effects on the city were lasting and it changed LeBron and his family's everyday life.

Goodyear factory,
Akron, Ohio

CHAPTER TWO

NOWHERE TO CALL HOME

When a kind neighbor offered Gloria and LeBron a place to sleep on her couch, it was a temporary solution to an immediate problem. They stayed on the neighbor's couch for a few months. Then they stayed at a cousin's place. They never imagined that they would spend six long years moving from one house or apartment to another. They stayed anywhere they were invited, until they wore out their welcome. They lived in one building that was so run-down, the city **evicted** everyone living there and tore it down.

Eventually, their travels took them to the Elizabeth Park projects, a gritty apartment complex near Akron's downtown. Gloria had a lot of friends they could stay with there. On the downside, there was also a lot of crime. LeBron's mind raced with worry as he lay awake in a strange bed at night, listening to the loud wails of sirens outside his window. He imagined violent gang fights taking place outside. In his **memoir** entitled *Shooting Stars*, LeBron described these as his "darkest days growing up."

Dark Days

In the spring of 1993, Gloria and LeBron moved five times in only three months. It was the most difficult time in LeBron's childhood. All the moving around was exhausting and made

Akron, Ohio

LeBron rode his bike to get away from bad situations.

getting to school—let alone doing homework or studying for tests—next to impossible. In the fourth grade, he missed 82 out of 160 days of school.

LeBron often rode his bike through the streets of Akron with nowhere in particular to go, and he always kept his head down. Many people mistook this for shyness. But LeBron was simply doing his best to stay out of trouble.

ALWAYS ON THE GO

Between the ages of five and eight,
LeBron and his mother moved a dozen
times! It's especially hard to make
friends when you keep moving around.
Although it was incredibly difficult
for him, LeBron found strength in the
source he always had: his mother. He
has said, "It's really all I cared about
when I was growing up, waking up and
knowing that my mom was still alive
and still by my side."

LeBron's mother wearing a jersey in support of her son

CHAPTER THREE

TEAM PLAYER

For the most part, LeBron succeeded in avoiding trouble. Although he was doing poorly in school, he didn't join a gang or sell drugs like some people around him. Despite the crime, LeBron has said that Akron was also the kind of place where people "found you and protected you and treated you like their own son even when you weren't."

But in order to stay on the right path, LeBron needed an even stronger **community**, which he found in organized sports. In 1994, LeBron joined the South Rangers, the local youth football team. Former NFL players and coaches often came out to watch the middle schoolers play, led by Coach Frankie Walker Sr. While coaching LeBron, Walker took note of both the boy's talent and his difficult home

Football was a good escape for LeBron.

life. Frankie Walker and
his wife, Pam, who already
had two daughters and a
son, invited LeBron to live
with them until Gloria found
a permanent place for them
to live.

Frankie Walker Sr.

A New Beginning

It was difficult for Gloria to be separated from
LeBron, but she knew the Walkers were able
to provide the stable home environment that
LeBron needed. They treated him like a son,
which meant chores, homework, and regular
meals for LeBron. Gloria was invited to spend
as much time at the house as she liked.

The Walkers quickly became like family to
LeBron. "The Walkers were disciplined, and
they plunged me right into that **discipline**," he
said of the life-changing experience. It paid

off. After years of struggling with schoolwork and absences, LeBron was able to maintain a B average and achieve a perfect attendance record during fifth grade.

Fifth grade was also the year LeBron started playing basketball.

A Rising Star

LeBron joined the Summit Lake Hornets, the youth rec league basketball team that Frankie Jr. played on and Frankie Sr. coached. LeBron's natural athleticism was immediately obvious to everyone. He was able to learn new plays with lightning speed. When Walker showed the team how to dribble and shoot with their opposite hand, LeBron was the only one able to use the new skill right away in the heat of competition. "You'd tell him something once," Walker recalled, "and then you'd see him do it in a game."

LeBron quickly became
a star for the Hornets.

LeBron also demonstrated incredible instinct and the skill of **anticipation**. He seemed to know what was going to happen on the court three or

LeBron (second from left)
with Coach Walker

four plays before it actually occurred. LeBron also had a remarkably positive attitude. Losing didn't make him mad; it made him

practice harder. He loved being part of a team, which provided him with another **surrogate** family. Coach Walker was so impressed that he made LeBron assistant coach of the younger grade team.

The qualities that promised to make a champion out of LeBron James were starting to take shape.

TO THE LEFT

Frank Walker Sr. may have taught LeBron the importance of discipline and routine, but he also taught him something else: the left-handed layup. Walker forced LeBron to practice his left-handed layups, encouraging him to be as good with his left hand as he was with his right. Frankie Sr. has said, "He used to cry about it. He used to say 'I can't do it.'" After winning games with last-second left-handed layups, LeBron has said, "I give credit to my little league coach, Frank Walker Sr. I've been doing that since I was eight years old."

LeBron using his left-handed
lay-up skills

LeBron wore No. 23, the famous number of Michael Jordan.

CHAPTER FOUR

A FAB START

By 1996, life was much better for the James family. Gloria had found a good job and was finally able to get a place of her own. Their two-bedroom apartment in Spring Hill, was only 300 square feet—but it was all theirs. LeBron, now almost twelve, moved back in with his mother and lived with her until he graduated from high school. He proudly wore the key to the front door around his neck. "Having your own key to your own crib—

Dru Joyce II

that's the greatest thing in the world," he told the *New York Times*.

LeBron joined a new basketball team: the Shooting Stars. Dru Joyce II, the coach of the national-level Amateur Athletic Union (AAU) team, could see that LeBron was a star. At only twelve years old, LeBron was already close to six feet tall, with a gift for controlling the action on the court. When LeBron played, it seemed as if everyone else was moving in slow motion. His coach knew that LeBron was good enough to play alone against five other players and win. But instead of putting a spotlight on LeBron, Dru helped him see the reward in helping his teammates to score rather than just dunking the ball himself.

THE FAB FOUR

During this time, LeBron built powerful friendships with some of his teammates. The coach's son, Dru III (known as "Little Dru"), Willie McGee, and Sian Cotton became LeBron's friends for life. Little Dru was the quiet one. Sian liked to joke around. Willie was mature for his age, like LeBron. Together, the four became like brothers on and off the court. They even gave their group a name: the Fab Four. And they lived up to their name. In the five years that the Fab Four played in the AAU, the Shooting Stars

Dru III

Willie McGee

Sian Cotton

The Fab Four

won more than two hundred games and six national championships.

LeBron received attention from his coach, teammates, and the fans of the Shooting Stars, and soon his ability earned him national

recognition. His name was known throughout the country as one of the best young players anyone had ever seen. As he prepared to go to high school, everyone in Akron assumed he would attend John R. Buchtel High School, which had a top-notch basketball program.

However, deciding where to attend high school was complicated for LeBron. The Fab Four didn't want to split up, but it was doubtful that Little Dru was tall enough to be on the team at Buchtel. LeBron faced a serious **dilemma**. Should he join the most competitive team, or stick with the guys? Would this be the end of the Fab Four?

EARNING HIS WINGS

The Shooting Stars expanded LeBron's world in many ways. He improved as a player and made lifelong friends. He also got to travel for the first time in his life. Competing in a national league meant the team went to other states for games, sometimes by plane. The first time LeBron had to fly for a national tournament in Salt Lake City, he was terrified. "He was scared stiff," Coach Dru told the *Akron Beacon Journal*. "He cried the entire time. He wanted his mother."

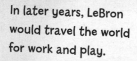

In later years, LeBron would travel the world for work and play.

LeBron at St. Vincent-
St. Mary High School, 2003

CHAPTER FIVE

RISING STAR

When LeBron started his first day of high school, Little Dru, Sian, and Willie were right by his side.

The Fab Four had made the collective decision to attend St. Vincent-St. Mary High School, which was known as "St. V." Many people were surprised by LeBron's choice. St. V was a small Catholic school with a reputation for strong academics, but it was not strong in basketball.

LeBron was in shock when he started school in the fall of 1999: culture shock. St. V had a dress code, a golf team, and without a scholarship tuition cost $8,000 a year, and many of his new classmates were white. "I had never spent any time with white Americans, and I didn't know anything at all about their culture," he told the *New York Times*. "It was a big **transition**."

At St. V, LeBron had a new coach, but he was a familiar face. St. V's Coach Keith Dambrot taught Sunday clinics at the local Jewish community center, which LeBron and the other Shooting Stars attended almost every weekend during eighth grade. Just as Coach Dru Joyce II had taught LeBron the value of passing the ball, Coach

Keith Dambrot

Dambrot kept the six-foot-four, 170-pound rising star humble by putting him in his place. "Coach Dambrot would yell at me, tell me all the time that I'm not as good as I think I am," LeBron said. "I needed that." LeBron practiced long and hard every day—a normal practice session included as many as 800 jump shots— and the work paid off. In his freshman year, the St. V "Irish" won the Ohio state championship. The Fab Four had done it again!

During LeBron's sophomore year, he worked hard to improve his skills. Out of twenty-eight games, the Irish lost only one game that year—they ended the season 27–1 and were state champs again. With a personal average of 25.2 points per game, LeBron was the first sophomore to receive Ohio's Mr. Basketball award, given to the top high-school player in the state. He was also named to *USA Today*'s All-American team, another first for a sophomore.

BETTER THAN THE REST

That summer, LeBron joined a basketball camp called Five-Star, which famous players like Michael Jordan, Moses Malone, Stephon Marbury, and Carmelo Anthony had all attended. Even at camp, LeBron stood out. Howard Garfinkel, the scout who started Five-Star in 1966, said he'd never seen anything quite like it. Usually Five-Star players were divided into two leagues by age. After only four games, Garfinkel decided LeBron's skills were far greater than the other players in his age group and suggested he move up to the league for older players. However, the loyal LeBron didn't want to leave his league team, and got permission from Garfinkel to play in both leagues. That meant he was in four games a day instead of two, and he still made it to the All-Star games for both leagues! Garfinkel said that no one had ever played in both leagues before.

TAKING NOTICE

Back in high school for his junior year, LeBron continued to draw attention. Standing six feet seven inches tall and weighing 225 pounds, LeBron had the height and the strength to push his skills to the next level. His high-school basketball games became major sporting events. As his fame grew, St. V's gym didn't have enough seats for everyone who wanted to watch LeBron and the Irish beat their competitors. Soon, the Irish started playing many of their home games at the University of Akron basketball court.

Famous NBA players like Kobe Bryant and Shaquille O'Neal, as well as professional scouts, came to check him out. One scout deemed him the best high-school player of all time. Everyone agreed that LeBron would be the first pick in the NBA draft if he left high school at the end of his junior year. Immediately, rumors

LeBron going
in for a slam dunk

LeBron and Shannon Brown sharing the MVP trophy at the Jordan Capital Classic, 2003

started to fly that he was going to quit school to join the pros before graduation. In February 2002, when LeBron was still in eleventh grade, he appeared on the cover of *Sports Illustrated* with the headline "The Chosen One." But LeBron made his graduation plans clear to the press when he said: "That is not going to happen. I can do more to get my brain and my game ready if I finish school."

FOOTBALL STAR

During his junior year, LeBron also played high-school football as a wide receiver. He was so good that he made the all-state team. But Gloria didn't want him to play. She was concerned that LeBron could hurt himself and risk his chance at a career in the NBA. Although he did quit football after his junior year, LeBron never lost his love for the game. In 2013, LeBron bought cutting-edge, all-black uniforms for St. V's football team.

LeBron and Dru at their high school graduation

CHAPTER SIX

UNDER THE MICROSCOPE

Senior year is a stressful time for many kids, and for LeBron, it was a pressure cooker. He still went to the movies with friends, played video games, ate big bowls of cereal for dinner, and had to clean his room. But at the same time, LeBron had basketball scouts breathing down his neck as well as companies asking him to sign **endorsement** deals as soon as he went into professional basketball. Endorsement deals are when companies pay people (usually celebrities or athletes) to put their names on, appear in commercials for, or help to design a product.

The more famous LeBron got, the more people watched and judged his actions. He had to be especially careful about the rules that banned student athletes from taking any money or gifts. LeBron knew just how seriously the **regulations** were enforced. He refused to sign any copies of his *Sports Illustrated* covers for strangers, because he knew copies could be sold on eBay for large sums of money.

However, in May 2002, he did accept a special invitation from the Cleveland Cavaliers to work out with its players. That broke with the policy stating that NBA teams are not to have contact with amateur players unless they are **eligible** to play professionally. Cavaliers coach John Lucas was suspended for the first

LeBron practiced with the Cleveland Cavaliers.

two games of the 2002–2003 season, and the team was fined $150,000.

UNDER FIRE

In January 2003, LeBron created his own controversy when he arrived at school in a customized Hummer H2, which was worth about eighty thousand dollars. He said it was a present from Gloria for his eighteenth birthday. The story was hard to believe. How could his mom afford to buy him such an expensive car? The press speculated that the car was a gift from a sporting goods company as an **incentive** to sign an endorsement. The accusations threatened LeBron's amateur athletic status and his chances of finishing the season with his high-school team. Two weeks after the initial accusations, Gloria shared copies of the paperwork for the bank loan she'd taken out to buy the car, proved LeBron's innocence, and the scandal died down.

A Hummer H2

Unfortunately, Gloria soon found herself defending her son again. In return for autographed pictures of himself, LeBron accepted a few vintage sports jerseys as a gift from the owner of a clothing store in Cleveland. Regulators said he couldn't finish his high-school season although the store owner insisted the jerseys were simply a thank-you gift. LeBron was heartbroken at being benched and letting his teammates down. "I love them to death and I can do nothing without my teammates," he said in an interview.

Gloria hired an attorney to fight the ruling, which was eventually reversed. LeBron came back to the court ready to win. He was so pumped during his first game back that he scored 52 points, the most he'd ever scored in a single game. The Fighting Irish became the first Ohio team to get to the finals four years

in a row. They won the state championship, and were ranked the number one high-school team in the country by *USA Today*.

BY THE NUMBERS

Although the Hummer H2 his mom bought him during his senior year got him in a lot of trouble, LeBron continued to enjoy the tricked-out ride long after he went pro. In 2007, the massive vehicle underwent a serious makeover on *Unique Whips*. The Speed Channel TV show outfitted the car with 28-inch custom rims, a touch-screen computer, a Sony PlayStation 2, a custom audio system, a bunch of TV monitors, and more. "I might as well live in here," James said on air. "All I need is a pillow and a blanket." Maybe so, but he didn't drive it much. When a Cleveland auto dealer put the infamous car up for auction on eBay in 2014 for $64,800, it only had 28,117 miles.

TV TIME

During LeBron's senior year, ESPN2 decided to broadcast one of his games—it was the first time a high-school game had been broadcast live in prime time. Twelve thousand people were in the stands at the Rhodes Arena to watch the Fighting Irish compete against the Oak Hill Warriors. With 31 points, 13 rebounds, and 6 assists, LeBron helped his team win 65-45.

The TV crews didn't bother LeBron.

Madison Square Garden

CHAPTER SEVEN

A ROOKIE IN NAME ONLY

By the time LeBron and Gloria arrived for the NBA draft at Madison Square Garden in New York City on June 26, 2003, he was already a multimillionaire. Everyone knew what was going to happen in the draft and that LeBron was going to be a huge pro basketball star. Nike was so certain of his future success that they made a deal worth a lot of money for LeBron to sell their sneakers right after he finished high school. Dressing the part,

LeBron wore an all-white ensemble with huge diamond earrings and a diamond watch to the draft.

For weeks leading up to the NBA draft, the world's biggest sneaker companies had been **wooing** the high-school senior in the hope he would sign an exclusive endorsement deal with them. Adidas chartered a private jet for LeBron and his friends to travel to a meeting in Los Angeles, and put them up at a Malibu mansion with a view of the Pacific Ocean. The only bummer was that the meeting took place during the same weekend as their senior prom, which he missed to take the meeting in L.A. Adidas's campaign was **elaborate**. They even bought billboards and bus signs with messages directly for LeBron! But despite Adidas's efforts, LeBron signed a seven-year contract with Nike worth a staggering $90 million. This deal trumped sneaker endorsements of the

past. When Michael Jordan signed his first endorsement deal with Nike in 1984, it was worth $7 million.

ROOT FOR THE HOME TEAM

The draft pick at the Garden was obvious,

LeBron's line of Nike sneakers has outsold the next most popular NBA star's sneakers by 6 to 1. In 2012, his line of sneakers earned Nike $300 million. He named one pair of sneakers after his first basketball team: the Nike LeBron 9 Summit Lake Hornets. The Nike Zoom LeBron VI has "Gloria" hidden in the midsole, while the Nike Air Max LeBron VII has an image of Gloria and LeBron on the tongue.

since LeBron was clearly number one. The lucky team that landed him was none other than his home state's Cleveland Cavaliers, who were then tied for the worst record in the NBA. Fans of the struggling franchise were counting on LeBron to turn things around. All eyes were on him. For his debut game of the

2003–2004 season against the Sacramento Kings, the Kings' press office gave out twice the normal number of press passes. When asked how LeBron, only eighteen, was handling the pressure, he answered, "As long as you've got friends, you've got nothing to worry about." With confidence that the Fab Four, his mom, and the rest of his close circle would always have his back, LeBron played his heart out during his first season. Although the Cavaliers didn't make the playoffs, he was named Rookie of the Year.

A NEW ROLE

Becoming a pro basketball player wasn't the only big change in LeBron's life. Eight days before the first preseason game of 2004–2005, his girlfriend, Savannah Brinson, gave birth to their son LeBron James Jr. LeBron missed three practices so that he could be with Savannah for the birth of his first child in Akron. Although he never grew up with a father, LeBron was thrilled to become one.

LeBron and Savannah had known each other since high school, although she went to a rival school. After meeting her at a football game, LeBron asked the pretty softball player and cheerleader to come to his school to watch one of his basketball games. She knew he really liked her after their first date at the Outback Steakhouse, because he later brought her the leftovers she forgot in his car. "He just wanted another excuse to come and see me," she said.

LeBron was interested in Savannah from the beginning.

USA, USA!

During the summer after his first NBA season, LeBron went to the Olympics in Athens, Greece, with the U.S. Men's Basketball Team as the youngest player ever to be on Team USA. Unfortunately he spent most of his time during the games on the bench—which might have had something to do with the team bringing home the bronze. Luckily, LeBron had another chance in Beijing during the 2008 Olympics, when the U.S. team went undefeated all the way to the finals, where they beat Spain to win a gold medal. In the London games of 2012, Team USA found itself up against Spain again in the final game, where LeBron had 19 points to win gold. During those three Olympics, LeBron made history by becoming the all-time leading scorer in U.S. Men's Basketball history.

London Olympic
Games, 2012

LeBron on the court, 2007

CHAPTER EIGHT

HERE COMES THE CAVALRY

In spite of a few winning seasons since the team's start in 1970, the Cavaliers had been on a losing streak for many years before LeBron's arrival. Over the next four years, LeBron helped the Cavaliers improve their record, and fan attendance at home games soared. Yet while LeBron was picked for the NBA All-Star Game every year he was with the team, the Cavs' failure to get to the championship finals was a constant disappointment to the team's managers.

Before the 2005–2006 season, the team hired Mike Brown as the new head coach and **acquired** several top-tier players through trades. The Cavs made the playoffs that year for the first time since 1998, but ended up losing in the second round to the Detroit Pistons. Meanwhile, LeBron continued to be a powerful leader on the court, becoming the youngest player to score 4,000 career points.

In the 2006–2007 season, the Cavs avenged their loss to the Pistons and made it all the way to the NBA Finals. Unfortunately, they were outmatched by the San Antonio Spurs, who swept the Cavs 4–0.

LeBron couldn't be upset over the loss for long. Early in the morning on the day of the last game, Savannah gave birth to their second child, named Bryce Maximus James. (Maximus is the name of the lead character in LeBron's favorite film, *Gladiator*.)

Savannah with their two children

But his ultimate goal of a league championship still seemed out of reach. In 2007–2008, the Cavs failed to make it to the Finals. But they made some key changes in the off-season, including adding an awesome point guard named Mo Williams.

A FRESH SEASON

With Mo and LeBron as a team, the 2008–2009 season would be one of the best for the Cavs, who finished 66–16, their best record ever. LeBron was a powerhouse all the way. After a game against the Milwaukee Bucks, during which he scored 55 points (including eight three-pointers), one teammate said that playing with him was "like watching a video game." He was again named MVP at the end of the season. But once again, the Cavaliers couldn't close the deal, and lost to the Orlando Magic in the Eastern Conference Finals.

The Cavs still lacked the support LeBron needed on the court, so the Cavaliers acquired Shaquille O'Neal in 2009. The NBA veteran helped bring the team to the championships the following year, but again they lost—this time to the Boston Celtics in the second round of the playoffs.

LeBron was named MVP, went to the All-Star Game, and became the youngest player ever to score 15,000 points in his career.

But none of that was enough. LeBron wanted to be a champion.

COVER BOY

Between 2002 and 2013, LeBron appeared on
the cover of *Sports Illustrated* twenty times.
Making the cover of the magazine, which is more
than fifty years old and has over three million
readers, is most athletes' dream. But LeBron had
no clue what an honor it was. "I didn't know till
I was like twenty-one years old how big *Sports
Illustrated* was," he said. "Then I was like, Wow! I
was pretty big in high school!" If he didn't learn
what a big deal *Sports Illustrated* was from the
other players in the NBA, then he might have
figured it out from how much autographed
copies of his 2002 cover cost collectors.
More than ten years later, an autographed
and framed copy of LeBron's first cover had a
starting bid of $475 on eBay!

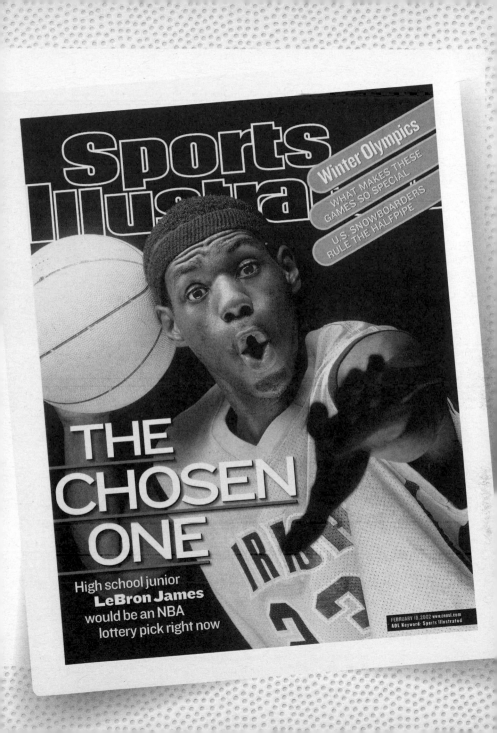

Sports Illustrated

Winter Olympics

WHAT MAKES THESE GAMES SO SPECIAL

U.S. SNOWBOARDERS RULE THE HALFPIPE

THE CHOSEN ONE

High school junior **LeBron James** would be an NBA lottery pick right now

FEBRUARY 18, 2002 www.cnnsi.com
AOL Keyword: Sports Illustrated

LeBron and his mother holding the 2009 MVP trophy

CHAPTER NINE

THE HEAT IS ON

Fans of the Cleveland Cavaliers were devastated by their team's loss to the Boston Celtics in the 2010 NBA playoffs. They also had bigger worries. LeBron's contract was up at the end of the season, making him eligible for free agency. In other words, he could play for any team he wanted. He could leave Cleveland.

Theories swirled as to what team LeBron would choose. Many assumed he would stay in Cleveland in order to finally win an NBA championship with the Cavs. Others guessed he would go to a bigger city like New York or Los Angeles.

On the evening of July 8, 2010, LeBron added to the suspense by appearing on a live television special called *The Decision*, which aired on ESPN. With the cameras rolling and basketball fans everywhere on the edge of their seats, LeBron announced: "In this fall— this is very tough—in this fall, I'm going to take my talents to South Beach and join the Miami Heat."

THE DECISION

Some 13 million viewers had tuned in to watch *The Decision*. And many of them were very unhappy about his choice. It was a very **controversial** decision, especially for his fans back home in Ohio, who were counting on LeBron for a championship title. They ripped

LeBron in his Miami Heat jersey

Cavaliers fans were outraged by LeBron's decision to leave their team.

up LeBron posters in the streets, and some even set fire to the player's No. 23 jersey. In a public letter, the team's majority owner Dan Gilbert called LeBron "selfish" and "heartless."

LeBron had **agonized** over the decision. He didn't just want to be a star. He wanted to be a champion. And in the Miami Heat, he saw just that: a collection of players with the potential to win multiple championships. Yet when reporter Jim Gray asked LeBron about leaving his hometown team, LeBron admitted, "It's very tough, because you feel like you let a lot of people down . . . I never wanted to leave Cleveland. And my heart will always be around that area."

A NEW START

But LeBron was embraced by a new family in Miami. In particular, he found friends in two other Heat players: Chris Bosh and Dwyane

Chris Bosh

Dwyane Wade

Wade. It was similar to his high-school days, when LeBron had such incredible chemistry with his teammates at St. V. Only instead of the Fab Four, in Miami it was the "Big Three."

As the 2010–2011 season got under way, the Heat struggled to find its rhythm, though LeBron was playing well. It was going to take the team some time to come together. Eventually, the Heat hit its stride and made it to the playoffs. They breezed through the early rounds, defeating the Philadelphia 76ers, the

Boston Celtics, and the Chicago Bulls. But then the Heat lost in the championship to the Dallas Mavericks. It was a stinging loss for LeBron and the team.

The media was quick to blame LeBron. They said that the pressure was getting to him and that his team wasn't behind him. And of course, fans in Cleveland delighted in the Heat's defeat.

THE GIFT OF GIVING

Many people criticized LeBron for dramatizing his team choice on TV in *The Decision*. But LeBron has said that his motivation for making his announcement on national TV was driven by his desire to help others. The $2.5 million that LeBron and his business team made from selling ad time went to the Boys & Girls Clubs. "When I found out I had an opportunity to do that for those kids, it was a no-brainer for me," LeBron said afterward. Giving back has always been on LeBron's agenda. The year he went pro, he started the LeBron James Family Foundation, which gives aid to single-parent families. In 2005, he donated $200,000 to efforts to help victims of Hurricanes Katrina and Rita. He pledged $1 million to the foundation ONEXONE, a global organization that supplies children with food, clean water, health care, and education. He has donated thousands of backpacks filled with school supplies to the Ohio school system, and sporting equipment to local community centers.

LeBron James Family
Foundation event in Florida

LeBron holding the
2012 MVP trophy

CHAPTER TEN

A CHAMPION AT LAST

The 2011–2012 NBA season offered LeBron yet another chance at his dreams. He had been working hard to improve his game and he was determined to win the championship. Unfortunately, the start of the season was delayed by a lockout as the league's owners and players struggled to agree on a new contract.

The season finally got under way on December 25, 2011, reducing the number of games from 82 to 66. For LeBron, it was a long and painful wait. But once play finally resumed, he was ready to go. The Heat finished the season with a 46–20 record, good enough for a first-place finish in the division.

PLAYOFF PRESSURE

The Heat started the playoffs against the New York Knicks, beating them easily, four games to one in the five-game series. Next up was the Indiana Pacers, who were coming off a very strong season. The Heat took Game 1, but then Chris Bosh suffered an abdominal strain and had to be sidelined, possibly for the rest of the season. The Pacers then won Games 2 and 3, throwing the Heat for a loop.

The pressure was on LeBron. Would he buckle under the weight or would he rise to the occasion? LeBron answered his critics with one of the greatest games of his career,

LeBron in action, 2012

tallying 40 points, 18 rebounds, and 9 assists in the pivotal Game 4. The last player to post those kinds of numbers in the playoffs was Elgin Baylor, NBA Hall of Famer, in 1961! It was a huge performance and a huge win, giving the momentum back to the Heat. They took the next two games and moved on to the Eastern Conference Finals, where they beat the Boston Celtics.

WE ARE THE CHAMPIONS

That sent LeBron back to the championship, against the close-knit Oklahoma City Thunder that was playing at the top of its game, and was led by star forward Kevin Durant. The Thunder took Game 1 of the series thanks to Durant scoring 36 points. For a moment, it looked like LeBron and the Heat were going to fall short yet again. But that's when LeBron took over.

Even though he was suffering from bad leg cramps, LeBron never stopped pushing. The Heat took the next three games. In Game 5, with victory within reach, LeBron led the charge on offense as well as defense. The Heat won the championship! LeBron was unanimously voted the NBA Finals MVP. "I can finally say that I'm a champion, and I did it the right way," he would later reflect. "I didn't shortcut anything. You know, I put a lot of hard work and dedication in it, and hard work pays off."

Dwyane Wade, Chris Bosh, and LeBron show off their championship rings.

ROUND 2

LeBron's next question was: *What now?* He had spent his career striving for a championship, and he wanted to avoid a post-victory letdown. He worked even harder on his game in the off-season to prepare for a repeat in 2012. It paid off, with LeBron playing the best basketball of his life. The Heat dominated the league, ending the 2012–2013 season with a 66–16 record. At one point, they had won 27 games in a row.

The Heat opened the playoffs against the Milwaukee Bucks, sweeping the series with four straight wins. They won five games to beat the Chicago Bulls in the Eastern Conference Semifinals. In the Conference Finals, the Indiana Pacers gave the Heat more of a challenge, pushing the series to a decisive seventh game. But the Heat were victorious in the seventh game, with LeBron scoring an impressive 32 points.

In the 2013 NBA Finals, the Heat faced the incredibly tough San Antonio Spurs, which were led by Tim Duncan and Tony Parker. The momentum swung back and forth throughout the series, with the Spurs taking Games 1, 3, and 5, and the Heat winning Games 2, 4, and 6. Game 6, which some call the greatest game in NBA history, has been dubbed the "Headband Game" because LeBron lost his trademark headband on a dunk in the fourth quarter and played the rest of the game without it.

The Heat took on the Spurs again in Game 7, which was played in Miami. It was a chance for LeBron to capture another championship in front of the hometown crowd. He did not disappoint, scoring 37 points, including a 17-foot jumper in the closing seconds that sealed the victory for his team.

NBA Finals, 2012

BORN TO BE KING

Once again, LeBron was named the NBA Finals MVP. He later gave a short speech that went right to the heart of his long journey. "I'm LeBron James, from Akron, Ohio," he said. "From the inner city. I'm not even supposed to be here. That's enough."

LeBron is here, and he's here to stay. How many more championships will he win? How many more MVP awards? Only time will tell. But one thing is certain: There is no better player on the basketball court today.

WEDDING BELLS

LeBron proposed to his high-school sweetheart, Savannah Brinson, on New Year's Eve in 2011. In September 2013, they married in San Diego. LeBron wrote on Instagram, "When u have someone that's always there for you no matter the ups and downs in life, it makes it all worth living for!" Savannah obviously feels the same way. She has said, "I just love him so much. We're soul mates." Hundreds of guests gathered at San Diego's Grand Del Mar resort for the wedding, including LeBron's teammate Dwyane Wade and fellow NBA players Chris Paul and Carmelo Anthony.

LeBron enjoying a moment with his family

10 THINGS YOU SHOULD KNOW ABOUT LEBRON JAMES

1. LeBron was born on December 30, 1984, in Akron, Ohio.

2. He started playing organized sports when he was ten, first football and then basketball.

3. Between the ages of twelve and sixteen, LeBron won six national championships with the Shooting Stars, the team he played with in the Amateur Athletic Union league.

4. He attended St. Vincent-St. Mary High School, leading the team to three state championships.

5. LeBron was picked in the first round of the 2003 NBA draft by the Cleveland Cavaliers; he spent his first five seasons with the team.

6 He won gold medals with Team U.S.A. in the 2008 Beijing Olympics and the 2012 London Olympics.

7 In a nationally televised event known as *The Decision*, LeBron announced on July 8, 2010, that he would be moving from the Cleveland Cavaliers to the Miami Heat.

8 LeBron won his first NBA championship in the 2011–2012 season, when the Heat defeated the Oklahoma City Thunder. They repeated as champions in the 2012–2013 season, this time beating the San Antonio Spurs in the Finals.

9 He is a nine-time NBA All-Star, four-time NBA Most Valuable Player, and two-time NBA Finals MVP.

10 LeBron married his high-school sweetheart, Savannah Brinson, in 2013. They have two sons, LeBron James Jr. and Bryce Maximus James.

10 MORE THINGS THAT ARE PRETTY COOL TO KNOW

1 LeBron chose No. 23 for his Cavaliers jersey because 23 belonged to his favorite player, Michael Jordan, when he played for the Chicago Bulls. But LeBron prefers that comparisons to his hero end there. LeBron once tweeted, "I'm not MJ, I'm LJ."

2 LeBron has about thirty tattoos, including one of his mom's name on his arm. During high-school games, he had to cover it up with tape or bandages because tattoos aren't allowed on the court. His biggest tattoo says "Chosen 1" across his back.

3 LeBron was awarded the Most Valuable Player award at the Jordan Capital Classic in Washington, D.C., in 2003, but insisted that he share it with teammate Shannon Brown, because Brown played a key role in helping the team win.

4 LeBron and Kobe Bryant have both said in interviews that they were annoyed at how often they had been compared to each other in the media when LeBron was in high school.

5 Kobe Bryant gave LeBron a pair of sneakers as a gift when he came to see him play in high school.

Kobe Bryant and LeBron play in the All-Star Game.

6 LeBron has been on the cover of *Sports Illustrated* twenty times.

7 LeBron's Miami Heat jersey is the league's top seller, with more than 2.2 million sales to date—nearly a million more than the next best seller.

New York, 2014

8 LeBron's line of Nike sneakers has outsold the next most popular NBA star's sneakers by 6 to 1.

9 LeBron and Michael Jordan are the only two players ever to win the NBA League MVP, NBA Finals MVP, and an Olympic gold medal all in the same year.

10 LeBron fulfilled another dream when he hosted NBC's *Saturday Night Live* in 2007.

GLOSSARY

Acquired: to have gotten something so that you own it or have it

Agonized: experienced severe pain or suffering

Anticipation: a feeling of excitement about something that is going to happen

Community: a place and the people who live in it

Condemned: labeled as unfit for use

Controversial: causing a great deal of disagreement

Dilemma: a situation in which any possible choice has some disadvantages

Discipline: control over your own or someone else's behavior

Elaborate: complex and detailed

Eligible: having the right abilities or qualifications for something

Endorsement: showing support or approval of someone or something; payment exchanged for support and approval of products

Evicted: to have forced someone to move out of a place

Incentive: inspiration to do something

Memoir: a story of personal experience

Poverty: the state of being poor

Recognition: appreciation or acknowledgment of someone or something

Regulations: official rules or orders

Surrogate: one that serves as a substitute

Transition: a change from one form, condition, or place to another

Wooing: seeking, gaining, or bringing about

PLACES TO VISIT

Find your own inspiration from LeBron James by visiting places from his life, either online or in real life.

American Airlines Arena, Miami, Florida

aaarena.com

Naismith Memorial Basketball Hall of Fame, Springfield, Massachusetts

hoophall.com

The official Miami Heat NBA website

nba.com/heat

LeBron James's personal website

lebronjames.com

The LeBron James Family Foundation website

lebronjamesfamilyfoundation.org

BIBLIOGRAPHY

LeBron James (Revised Edition)(Amazing Athletes), Jeff Savage, Lerner Publications, 2012.

LeBron James (Sports Illustrated Kids: Superstar Athletes), Joanne Mattern, Capstone Press, 2011.

LeBron James: The Rise of a Star, David Lee Morgan, Jr., Gray & Company, 2003.

On the Court with . . . LeBron James, Matt Christopher, Little, Brown, 2008.

Shooting Stars, LeBron James and Buzz Bissinger, Penguin Books, 2009.

INDEX

Also Available: